HOW TO FIND YOUR FAMILY ROOTS

by
William Latham

JBG PUBLISHING
Los Angeles
Printed in the United States
All Rights Reserved

JBG PUBLISHING
849 North Sierra Bonita
Los Angeles, California 90046
Copyright 1988 JBG PUBLISHING

TABLE OF CONTENTS

CHAPTER ONE

INTRODUCTION

The Excitement of Genealogy

Have you ever wondered if one of your ancestors was a famous, important person? A President, or maybe even a King of another country? Perhaps your last name is Washington, and you've always fancied yourself as a distant relative of the father of our country. If you've shown a flair for painting or writing, maybe you've fantasized that your talent is really in your genes, coming from an ancestor with a name like Michelangelo or Shakespeare.

Yes, the heritage of each and every one of us is a fascinating thing. Who hasn't dreamed of origins, of people living in another place, in another time? Who hasn't seen an old photograph of a person that bore a striking resemblance to themselves, and thought, "What if . . . ?"

The science of genealogy can unlock these doors and answer such intriguing questions as these. In this book, I will show you how you can go back into history to find out just who you *really* are and where you came from. While I will primarily be concentrating on tracing your American roots, I will also offer some helpful hints on obtaining information from your ancestral homeland. And what's more, I'll show you how to do it in a simple, easy, and inexpensive manner.

Definition and History of Genealogy

The term, "genealogy," actually comes from two

Greek words, "genea," which means "race" or "family," and "logia," which means "science," or "study of." When we speak of the science of Genealogy, we are really talking about the study of the descent of a person or of a family.

The science of genealogy is as old as the Bible, which serves as the first written example of genealogy. Early civilizations like the Greeks, for example, showed a keen interest in genealogy—the works of Homer and the plays of Aeschylus and Euripedes prove this. Any way you look at it, however, interest in man's lineage is as old as civilized man himself.

One of the original uses of genealogy was to prove that a person was descended from either certain Gods and Goddesses or from particular Kings and Queens. Therefore, up until the 16th century, the science of genealogy was most often used by either rulers or the upper classes. In the 16th century, extensive written records began to be kept, thus making it far easier for ordinary citizens to trace back their lineage.

Your Goals and End Results

As you begin the task of unraveling the mystery that is your origin, you will learn a great deal about the history of both America and the World, geography, people and their lifestyles, and most importantly, about yourself: who you are and where you come from.

Ideally, you should be able to trace yourself back to the original paternal and maternal immigrants of your family. If you are able to do this, you will know your complete American genealogy and you should congratulate yourself—this is not an easy task and many people never get this far. If you are extremely fortunate, you will be able to trace back your lineage to the forefathers of your family's original immigrants, to those who were born and those who died in some far away country hundreds of years ago.

Most likely, though, you will be able to go back several generations, which is an accomplishment you should be very proud of. Why? Because you will have the satisfaction of knowing that you have done everything humanly possible to find your roots with the information available to you, and that you have set up a solid foundation for future generations who will also want to go back and search out their own roots. By providing a written record of your lineage now, you will give those who follow in your footsteps immeasurable joy in knowing just who they are and where they come from.

No matter how far back you are able to go, however, you have much ahead of you to look forward to. Anyone who enjoys a good mystery or a challenging crossword puzzle—and who doesn't—will find tracing a family tree to be an exciting experience. This search for your roots will take you through time and from exotic place to exotic place both on paper and in your imagination, and will give you a greater sense of just exactly how you fit into this giant web of people and places that we call the history of mankind.

But perhaps I am getting a little too serious here. The main thing you must keep in mind is to have fun with your search. Because it's not about how far back you are able to go or how complete a family history you are able to put together. No, it's really about getting in touch with relatives you haven't talked to in a long time or perhaps have never even met. It's about finding long lost mementos and hearing old family tales that have been buried in the memories of your older relatives for years and years because nobody was ever truly interested enough to ask them to tell these stories. It's about all this and much more . . . so what are you waiting for? Let's begin your search for your family roots!

CHAPTER TWO

THE HISTORY OF IMMIGRANTS

Crossing the Ocean

Beginning with those who sailed to America aboard the Mayflower in 1620, the first immigrants who came to our country were primarily from England. In the early part of the 18th century, the Germans, Scottish, and Irish began crossing over, and by the end of the 1700s, there were close to five million people living in the United States, most of whom were from these four original countries. (There were also ¾ of a million black African slaves living in the United States at this time, but because they did not come here of their own choosing, they were not included in immigration figures.)

By the mid-1800s, people from all over the world, including Ireland, France, Switzerland, China, and Japan, began immigrating to the United States. And between 1880 and the early part of the 20th century, over 15 million southern and eastern Europeans came to sample and savor the riches of America.

It was precisely these "riches," better known as the "profit motive," that drove immigrants towards America. But religious persecution, political oppression and a host of other reasons—including broken hearts, wanderlust, and the attraction of the unknown—also played a part in the decisions people made to come to the land of opportunity.

Virtually every European immigrant left from one of two sea ports which were located in Germany—

at Hamburg and Bremen. These ports were very seedy and there were many wicked and evil people looking to take advantage of the frightened and lonely travelers. Perhaps it is partly because of this that most immigrants arrived in the United States with less than 25 dollars in their pockets.

As far as the journey across the ocean was concerned, it was, in the early days anyway, an extremely rough and uncomfortable trip. A typical passenger would be crammed into a tiny cabin with perhaps a half dozen other travelers. Rarely would anybody ever complete the whole journey without having at least one bout of seasickness.

Some days a ship might sail at a rate of as much as eight miles an hour, but other times the passengers could end up further from their future home than they were when they had awoken at dawn.

The length of the voyages varied from a little over a month to well over four months, bringing even more uncertainty to the already frightened travelers. At times, groups of ships would sail together, and members of the crew as well as passengers could visit other ships. Other times, however, days would pass without another ship in sight.

Many dangers, ranging from mean-spirited Pirates who roamed the open seas, to fierce storms which pounded the planks of the ships, also contributed to the overall hardship of the journey. But when all was said and done, once the immigrants set foot on American soil, they forgot the troubles that the trip had wrought, and looked forward to a new beginning and a new lease on life.

Before Ellis Island was built in 1892, immigrants were processed at Castle Garden, located at the far tip of Manhattan. Asian immigrants used to be processed at the Pacific Mail Steamship Company warehouse in San Francisco, but after 1910 they were welcomed at Angel Island in San Francisco Bay.

Once landed on the east coast of mid-17th century America, immigrants might take the King's Highway to Philadelphia, Norfolk, Virginia, or even as far south as Charleston, South Carolina. In later years, an immigrant could grab a stage coach in Philadelphia and take the Great Road out west towards Kentucky.

By the middle of the 1800s, roads began reaching further and further into the South and the West, taking new citizens to exotic far off places like New Orleans, Santa Fe, and throughout California. While the roads were tough, and the journey was rough, our forefathers bit the bullet and not only survived but triumphed with a dignity and a pride that has since gone on to be associated with the word, "American."

CHAPTER THREE

GETTING STARTED

Organizing Your Research Material

As you begin searching out your family roots, you will undoubtedly begin to gather a great deal of material, ranging from charts and documents to mementos and family photos. In order to keep track of everything, it is imperative that you put together some type of filing system. If you do not do this, you will end up with a morass of notes and papers, scattered about everywhere, making it virtually impossible for you to find necessary items which could be crucial to continuing your search.

Before getting into the particulars of a filing system, let me first go over the major documents which you will be working with. These are the Pedigree Charts (with coding system), the Family Work Sheets, the Individual Work Sheets, and the Individual Questionnaires.

Pedigree Charts (See figure 1)

A pedigree is the record of a line of ancestors. The first pedigree chart you will work with will go back five generations, to approximately the middle of the 1800s. As you move along in your search, you will be filling out the pedigree chart to mark your progress. It's probably a good idea to fill out this chart in pencil, in order to facilitate any changes you may have to make as you go along.

There is a basic, standard format which any genealogist, professional or amateur, follows

Figure 1: Pedigree Chart (4 Generation)

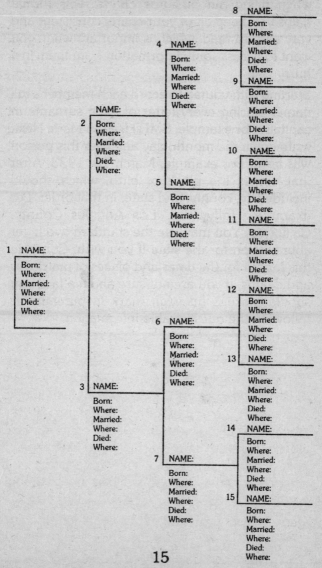

when filling out pedigree charts. This format helps you keep all of your charts consistent and very easy to read, which is important when you want to access some information from them in a hurry.

Starting with yourself, record each member's full name, placing every letter of each surname in capitals. For example, SMITH, John Mark. Next, write down the month, day and year this person was born. For example, March 18, 1933. After that comes the place of birth, which should include city, county, and state, in that order. For example, Hollywood, Los Angeles County, California. You may use the standard two letter abbreviation for the state if you wish. Continue this format for the dates and places of marriages and deaths. If you are not sure about a fact, you should place a question mark in parentheses following the questionable information.

Coding System

When filling out pedigree charts, you should assign each member a code number. Then, all materials which relate to individual family members will be filed under this same number. The easiest way to go about doing this is to begin with yourself, assigning the number 1 to your name. Number two will then go to your father, number 3 to your mother and so on. To further facilitate your records, only assign even numbers to males, and odd numbers to females. Therefore, number 4 will be your paternal grandfather (your father's father), number 5 your paternal grandmother (your father's mother), number 6 your maternal grandfather (your mother's father), number 7 your maternal grandmother (your mother's mother), etc. While this may initially seem to be slightly confusing, in the long run you will find that it actually makes all of your record keeping exceedingly clear and concise.

Individual and Family Work Sheets (See figures 2 and 3)

Along with your pedigree chart, these work sheets are your bread and butter, the primary tools which you will continually be working with. Filling out these sheets, as you can see, is relatively simple. There are one or two things to keep in mind however. First, while two and three marriages per individual is not all that common in the late twentieth century, in earlier times you will undoubtedly come across many family members who were married more than once, primarily because the much rougher and tougher lifestyles (along with the lack of modern medical research) often led to early deaths of one partner or another. Therefore, make sure you have ample space on your work sheets for such matters. Secondly, make sure that if a certain individual did have children with different marriage partners, that you keep a separate family group sheet for each marriage.

Most importantly, you must be extremely accurate when placing any information onto these work sheets. Any error could prove to be extremely costly, leading you into hours of research which will ultimately prove to be thoroughly needless and unwarranted. If, for instance, you place a wrong first name for one of the children, you could begin searching somebody's life who isn't even a member of your family. Therefore, always be sure to check and double check your facts and figures.

FIGURE 2: INDIVIDUAL WORK SHEET

Code Number: _____

Name: _____

Date of Birth: _____

Place of Birth: _____

Date of Death: _____

Place of Death: _____

Date of Marriage: _____

_____

_____

Place of Marriage: _____

_____

Name and Code Number
of Spouse: _____

_____

_____

Name and Code Number
of Father: _____

Name and Code Number
of Mother: _____

Occupation: _____

_____

_____

Places of Residence:
City   County   State   Dates
_____

_____

_____

Misc. Information:_____

_____

_____

FIGURE 3: FAMILY WORK SHEET

Husband's Name and
Code Number: _____

Wife's Maiden Name and
Code Number: _____

Date and Place
of Marriage: _____

Children:

Name	Birth Date/Place	Death Date/Place
_____	_____	_____
_____	_____	_____
_____	_____	_____
_____	_____	_____

Name	Name of Spouse	Marriage Date/Place
_____	_____	_____
_____	_____	_____
_____	_____	_____
_____	_____	_____

Places of Residence:

City	County	State	Dates
_____	_____	_____	_____
_____	_____	_____	_____

Misc. Information: _____
_____
_____

Filing System

Now we come to the final portion of the "setting up" period of your search for your family roots, namely the aforementioned filing system. While the filing of individual work sheets will simply follow a straight ahead numerical system—1, 2, 3, 4, 5, 6, . . .—the numbering system of your family work sheets will be slightly more complicated. Because each family work sheet is tagged with the code number of the husband (or head of the family), the numerical sequence will go 2, 4, 6, 8, 10 . . . (with the possible addition of number 1 if the genealogist himself is the head of a family). In summation, every single person who is placed on the pedigree chart will have an individual work sheet, but only heads of families will have family work sheets which correspond with their code number.

In addition to the individual and family work sheet files, I also recommend that you keep a miscellaneous file. Into this file will go smaller files, arranged by code numbers, which contain photographs, diaries, wills, newspaper clippings and anything else which pertains to a certain family member. This file is absolutely essential in order to ensure that you don't end up with piles of bits and pieces of information.

Now let's go through and see how your filing system and work sheets will operate. Let's say that you want to look up all the information that you have collected about your paternal grand-father (your father's father). To begin with, you will notice that on the pedigree chart, he has been assigned the code number of 4. You would then go to the individual work sheet numbered 4, the family work sheet which is also numbered 4, and the miscellaneous file which, obviously, is also marked with the number 4.

If, for instance, you wanted to look up your paternal grandfather's brothers and sisters, you would go to the family work sheet that is numbered 8. Why? Because, as you can see from the pedigree chart, your paternal grandfather's father has been assigned the number 8, and therefore all information about your grandfather's brothers and sisters will be contained on the family work sheet which corresponds with your grandfather's father's code number, or number 8. As you can see, this system is efficient and fairly simple to follow once you get going.

And that's exactly what you are now prepared to do. With an excellent record-keeping system at your disposal, you are now ready to plunge ahead into the wonderful and exciting world of "ancestor hunting." So, with this out of the way, let's go . . .

CHAPTER 4

LAST NAMES:
THE STARTING
POINTS
OF YOUR SEARCH

Origins and Meanings

While an individual's last name will rarely if ever solve an especially difficult search for a family member's origin, it can offer insights into such things as place of birth, occupation of the father or other relative of the individual, religion, cultural ties, class status, and even physical features.

It is estimated that there are over 1.5 million last names currently in use in the United States today. Despite the tremendous amount of immigrants who have brought vast numbers of Western and Eastern European names into the country, the most common names in America—Smith, Jones, Johnson, Brown, etc.—are virtually the same as they were around the time of the American Revolution.

Why is this? Basically because immigrants to this country changed their name when they entered the United States, in an attempt to Americanize their names. For instance, a French name such as Boulanger would often be changed to read simply Baker.

This, in turn, leads us into our next point of discussion: occupational names. Names such as Farmer, Fisher, Shepherd, and Miller were originally derived from the occupation of the person who owns such a name. This can often serve as a clue when searching the background of a certain ancestor, particularly in families where the same occupation was inherited by male members of the family, from generation to generation. Once you have traced your American lineage, and make the leap back overseas, you will undoubtedly come across non-English names from which your name (or your ancestor's) was ultimately derived. Any dictionary of names should be able to help you translate such names.

Last names can also be derived from nicknames, which will provide clues as to physical or personality characteristics of a particular ancestor. For instance, Longfellow was usually assigned to someone who was very tall or thin, while Reid went to an individual who had red hair, freckles, or a particularly hot tempered personality.

Finally, there are names which are formed by way of patrynomics. These are names which have derived from one's father. Such names point out that someone was the son or descendant of a particular person. For example, MacGregor is Scottish for "the son of Gregory," while Mendelssohn is German for the "son of Mendel." In English, one sees patrynomics at work in the last names of Johnson, Jackson, Peterson, and so on.

Last names are certainly far from being the most important clue which you will come across as you search for your family roots. Why, you may wonder, did I choose to begin with last names in our discussion of how to actually go about finding your family roots? Because it is a valuable lesson on the importance of being creative and using every available resource that is at your disposal.

You must be able to keep enough of an open mind to find that *one* clue, that *one* valuable piece of information, that solves a riddle and allows you to bring your search to yet another succeeding generation instead of stopping right then and there. ALWAYS BE CURIOUS.

CHAPTER FIVE

YOU AND YOUR FAMILY: YOUR MOST IMPORTANT RESOURCES

Begin With Yourself

When beginning your search for your family roots you must commence the hunt with an examination of yourself; you are the basic building block, the foundation as it may be, of the vast sculpture that will ultimately grow to be your family tree. Besides, you are obviously the easiest subject you have to research!

One thing to be aware of, however, is the importance of accurate information at this level of your search. Any wrong information on your part at this point could lead you on an erroneous path that will take you far from where you want to be.

You can start by filling out the pedigree chart as far back as you can possibly go with the knowledge you have at your immediate disposal, and then move onto your own individual work sheet and then to your or your father's family work sheet. Go as far back as you can possibly go, but keep in mind that you shouldn't put down any information that you *think* is correct. Unless you are absolutely positive about a fact, always check it out with one or more references before assuming it to be true.

You may have the urge to skip this portion of the research process, mistakenly thinking that you know it so well that you can write it all down at any time. But that is the wrong attitude to take at this point. Instead you should welcome the opportunity to get some valuable practice in research itself, recording facts and even verifying them in some cases.

Additionally, you must ask yourself why you are doing all of this to begin with. Remember, beside putting together a family history for yourself, you are also helping countless future generations of your descendants who will greatly appreciate the work you accomplished. They will want to know about you just as you want to know about some of your ancestors.

That is why it is also important to write down family anecdotes, accomplishments, quirks . . . in general, anything that strikes you as being interesting in any way. If all you record are simple facts such as birth dates and place names, you will end up with a very dry, fairly boring family history. On the other hand, little slices of life, sad and funny tales about family members, etc., will help to make your final family history an exciting, fascinating report to read.

Whenever you need check on some facts, try to go to the person who is still living who was closest to the person whose facts are in question. If, for example, you wanted to find out something about your great paternal grandfather's brothers and sisters, you could go to your paternal grandfather or one of his brothers or sisters to find out the names. If your grandfather and his brothers and sisters are no longer living, you could go to your father or one of your aunts or uncles.

Always remember to go as close to the source in question as possible when trying to verify facts. And just simply work towards yourself from that point onwards, from generation to generation. Only after you have exhausted your living sources should you turn to printed sources of information, which I will discuss in the following chapters.

Interviewing Your Living Family Members In Person

By beginning with live sources, you will save time, energy and just as importantly, you will have more fun! Talking with various relatives of yours will enable both of you to get to know each other better. In cases involving family members with whom you are not on good terms, ask another family member who knows both of you well to do the interviewing for you—but remember that this can only be considered second hand information.

After you have contacted your relative by mail or by phone, informed them of your project and your desire to interview them, and set up a time which is *convenient for the interviewee,* there are a few guidelines to follow to make sure you get a good, fun, and factual interview. Here they are:

1) Try to conduct the interview in a one on one setting. If another relative would like to be present at the interview, by all means allow him to do so, for many times, two

people talking about the past are able to trigger memories within each other.

2) Bring a tape recorder if at all possible. Small, portable tape recorders are relatively inexpensive, and their built in microphones are unobtrusive and non-intimidating. Plus, you'll have a permanent record of the whole conversation, including your relative's voice on tape, for succeeding generations to hear.

3) Have a list of questions to ask written down on a sheet of paper. When writing the questions down, try to write them in a way so that one question leads into the next. For instance, if you want to know about one relative in particular, keep all of your questions about this relative—when he was born, where he lived, etc.—together, so that the interview does not jump back and forth from person to person, place to place, and decade to decade.

4) LISTEN. This is the most important thing you can remember to do during an interview. Let the interviewee talk himself out. Never interrupt, and don't assume someone has finished just because they pause for a moment. Always wait for the person to tell you they are finished, or wait for a five or ten second silence before you ask your next question. If a relative seems to be wandering, talking about things you haven't asked him

31

about, by all means let him talk. It is very likely that he'll come up with an interesting fact or insight about your roots.

5) Phrase your questions in a manner that avoids any bias on your part. For instance, instead of asking, "Your Uncle Ralph was born in New Orleans, right?" You should say, "Where was your Uncle Ralph born?"

6) Don't make the interview last too long. One hour or so should be plenty of time, with two hours being the maximum amount of time you should impose on your subject. By all means, arrange for a second or even third interview if necessary, keeping in mind that two one and a half hour interviews is far more pleasurable and productive than one three hour interview.

7) Finally, please treat these situations as *conversations* rather than a more formal interview. The more relaxed you keep the meeting, the more fun both you and the interviewee will have.

Interviewing by Mail

Many times it is difficult to arrange a live interview because of money and/or geographical considerations. In such cases, you should try to interview your subject by mail. The first thing to do is to write up a cover letter. Here is an example of a good cover letter:

Dear Aunt Violet,

I am presently writing a complete history of our family. So far it has been a tremendously exciting challenge, made much easier by all of the help I have received from my relatives, both close and distant, who have provided me with loads of facts and stories in order to help me in my search.

I would be extremely grateful if you too could offer your help. I have sent along an individual work sheet and a family work sheet, and I would appreciate it if you would take the time to fill these out as best you can. I have also sent along a few questions for you to answer, and would be thankful if you could answer these for me, too.

When I am finished with this project, I plan on making copies for everyone in the family to own, and I'll be sure that you are one of the first to receive it.

All best wishes,

(your name)

PS—If you have any family records (diaries, bibles, photos, birth and death certificates, etc.) that you could possibly send me so that I may make a photocopy of them, I would be eternally grateful.

Along with your cover letter, you should include a brief questionnaire, with direct, to-the-point questions. Keep the number of questions you ask to a reasonable number, perhaps 12 at the most, or else you might discourage your potential source. Additionally, you should include a blank individual work sheet and a blank family work sheet. Finally, make sure you include a stamped, self-addressed envelope for their convenience.

Family Records as Sources of Information

When visiting or interviewing an older relative, ask if you may look at any family records he may have saved. If possible, try to gain access to attics and cellars, where things from the past have been simply packed away or discarded. I can almost guarantee that such searches will provide you with a storehouse of information. Here is what to look for:

Family Bibles—Early American tradition stipulated that the head of the family record all vital family information inside of the family bible, usually on the inside of the front cover or the first one or two pages. When checking out this information, always compare the publication date of the bible with the date of entry or date of birth of the person who recorded the information. This way, you'll be able to tell if the material was entered after the fact, or if it is indeed first hand information.

Diaries—While these will rarely provide you

with hard core facts, they will give you a unique insight into the cultural and intellectual history of a certain period of time.

Books—Books are a surprising fountain of information, as they often contain old letters, love notes, calling cards, newspaper clippings, and an assortment of other bits and pieces of information within their covers.

Letters—An extremely valuable source, not only for the contents of the letters themselves, but for what's on the outside of the envelope: addresses, return addresses, postmarks, and dates.

Family Records—Wills, deeds, birth and death certificates, passports, armed forces papers, college diplomas, contracts, mortgages, church records, health papers ... if it's a legal document of any kind, it most likely contains information that you can use.

Miscellaneous Items—Silverware, tea pots, quilts, jewelry, watches ... almost anything that can contain an inscription is worth taking a look at. You never know ...

CHAPTER SIX

THE TREMENDOUS RICHES OF LIBRARIES

The Library of the Church of Jesus Christ of Latter-Day Saints (LDS)

As any genealogist worth a grain of salt knows, the LDS library in Salt Lake City (along with their regional branches across the United States) has the most comprehensive collection of genealogical records in the world. Every year, this church spends millions and millions of dollars on research. Why? Because their religious doctrine stipulates that all members of the church maintain a thorough and accurate record of not only their immediate family, but of their ancestors as well.

Now, you may be wondering why I am telling you about this, especially if you have no affiliation with the church. Well, with upwards of 75 million records of ancestors in their vaults, there is a very good chance that the records of many of your relatives, whether or not they were in the church themselves, are contained within this massive library.

The best news, however, is that the LDS allows anyone, regardless of religious affiliation, to use their facilities. This means that all of the records of births, deaths, marriages, etc., which are contained on their microfilm files are all available for your perusal.

Obviously, the best way to utilize the LDS library is to take a trip to Salt Lake City and go through their microfilms yourself. If this is not possible for you to do, the next best thing is to visit one of the more than two hundred regional LDS libraries spread out across the United States. In such libraries, you won't find as much material as you would at the Salt Lake City branch, but you will gain access to a variety of records, and the staff at these regional libraries will be more than happy to order anything you need from the main library for a nominal charge.

The other option you have if you can not make it to Utah, is to take advantage of the LDS library's Pedigree Research Survey. For a small fee, one of the library's expert researchers will provide you with LDS records of one line of your family. You will receive a copy of your Family Work Sheet, suggestions for future research, and the names and addresses of other distant relatives of yours who are also working on putting together a Family History.

In order to get a survey done on your family, simply write to the Pedigree Research Survey, Suite 1006, 54 East South Temple St., Salt Lake City, Utah 84111. They will send you all the necessary information. You can also go to your local branch of the LDS library and ask them for information.

What to Ask Librarians by Mail

Once you have established which line of your family you are going to search first, and which area of the country you will begin with, you should contact a library from that region in order to obtain facts, records, or any other information which will be helpful to you as you search for your family roots.

When you write to any library, there are certain guidelines you should follow:

1) Keep your questions brief and to the point. Always give the full name of the person in question, the dates of his birth and death (if known, approximate if you don't know), and the name of the city and county he was born and/or lived in (again, if you don't know the exact name of the town, then give the librarian as much information as you have).

2) Ask about books on local history which might contain information about the ancestor in question.

3) Ask if there is already a family history on file at the library. Chances aren't that great, but you never know; maybe one of your earlier ancestors had the same interest in your family as you do.

4) Ask if there are any other people or history/ genealogical societies in the area who you should contact.

5) Always include a stamped, self-addressed envelope, and always offer to pay for any photocopying or other office expenses.

6) Never plan on having a librarian do every-

thing for you, such as filling out your work sheets. The more you keep your questions simple and small in number, the greater your chances for receiving valuable information.

The Library of Congress

The Library of Congress is the home of the largest collection of published family histories in the United States. The tens of thousands of books are alphabetized according to family name, making it fairly simple for you to conduct your research.

If you can't visit the Library of Congress in person, you can find out if there is a published history of your family name by writing to The Library of Congress, Science and Technology Division, Washington D.C. 20540. If there is such a published history, the staff at the Library will photocopy it for you for a moderate fee.

CHAPTER SEVEN

LOCAL AND STATE RECORDS

Primary Sources

In the world of researching, there are basically two types of sources: primary and secondary. Most of the sources we have discussed up to this point have been secondary sources, information that is not officially recorded, but is rather reported via a secondhand source, i.e. a story from a relative, a diary, entries in a family bible, etc.

It is now time to look at primary sources of information—such as local and state records, which can be categorized into two sections: criminal and civil. Criminal records are self-explanatory, and will most likely not be used by you during your search. Civil records, on the other hand, are the genealogist's goldmine. Civil records are divided into three categories: vital, probate, and land records. Along with providing you with information you have not been able to discover throughout the early portion of your search, these records will enable you to verify any fact you feel may be suspect.

Beginning Your Search of Local and State Records

Your first step will be to figure out when and where the particular ancestor you are researching did something that would cause him to be entered into the official records. This action could be something as significant as a birth, death, or marriage, or something more trivial like a land purchase.

Once you are fairly certain that records of your ancestor are located in a particular city or county, your next decision is whether to search out the record by mail or in person. As discussed in chapter 5, it is always preferable to conduct your research in person, but if this is not possible, then try writing a friendly, concise letter containing your request to the courthouse where you believe the record is located. While courthouse clerks are usually overloaded with work, there is a decent chance you will find one who can answer your request.

Normally, the person to either visit or write to is known as the "clerk of the court" or the "recorder of deeds." Generally, most of the records you will be searching for are located in the courthouses of the individual towns themselves, however, in many southeastern states, records are often filed in the State Archival Depository.

Vital Records

These records are primarily used to either find out or double check the date and place of your ancestor's birth, death, or marriage. There are many ways to go about locating these documents.

First, you can either write or visit the local courthouse where you think such records will be located. Second, for birth and death records after the last quarter of the 19th century, you can write to the U.S. Government Printing Office, Superintendent of Documents, Washington D.C. 20402 and request the brochure entitled "Where to Write for Birth and Death Certificates." This will tell you—state-by-state—what records are available, how much they cost, and where to write in order to receive them.

Third, you can consult the "WPA List of Vital Statistical Records" in your local library, which contains a state-by-state listing of information on where to locate vital records which were catalogued by the Works Progress Administration in the 1930s.

Finally, for information on Marriage or Divorce records from the 20th century, write to the U.S. Government Printing Office, Superintendent of Documents, Washington D.C. 20402, and request the brochures, "Where to Write for Marriage Records," and/or "Where to Write for Divorce Records."

Probate Records

Probate records are perhaps the most valuable pieces of information available to you as you search for your family roots. While there are many types of probate records, the main one you'll be concerned with is the last will and testament. Technically, the testament is concerned with the disposal of land, while the will primarily deals with an individual's personal property.

During your search you are likely to come across both written and oral (or nuncupative) wills. Oral wills were more common in earlier centuries, when many people did not know how to write, and writing utensils were not always readily available. Both types of wills are valid.

While searching through last will and testament records, you should also be on the lookout for any other probate records which might be contained in the same file. Litigation records, petitions, letters of testimony . . . there is a wealth of information pertaining to your ancestor and his immediate and/or distant relatives in such files, and careful research on your part could turn up an immense amount of material that will be beneficial as you search for your family roots.

When writing to a county clerk requesting a copy of a last will and testament, you might find that you can only receive an "abstraction," or parts of the document, rather than the whole will itself. In such cases, be sure to ask for the following information:

1) The name of the person who's will it is, the cause of his death, and the place where he was living at the time of his death.

2) The name of every person mentioned in the will and their relationship to the deceased.

3) A list of the property that was bequeathed.

4) The names of all witnesses and executors.

5) A description of any other useful information contained within the document itself, including seals and signatures.

Land Records

Land records include deeds, leases, mortgages, contracts . . . basically anything that has to do with the buyer and selling of land. The most important type of land record for your purposes is the "multiple-grantor deed," which lists all sales of a deceased land-owner's property by his children. This document will include the names and birth dates of both the children and their spouses, from the oldest to the youngest child in the family.

When checking out land deeds, look to see how the owner of the property acquired the piece of land, since there is a good possibility that he received it from an ancestor, which will provide you with another piece of your family history puzzle. Likewise, one piece of property is often passed down from generation to generation, and as such, one deed could provide you with all the information you need to complete a certain family work sheet.

CHAPTER EIGHT

UTILIZING FEDERAL GOVERNMENT RECORDS

The National Archives

On the Pennsylvania Avenue side of the National Archives building in Washington D.C., there is an inscription that reads, "The heritage of the past is the seed that brings forth the harvest of the future." This should give you a clue as to just how valuable the records stored here are for anyone who is searching for their family roots.

In the National Archives as well as other institutions located in our nation's capitol—the Smithsonian, the Library of Congress, the Immigration and Naturalization Service, etc.—there is an immense amount of information available to any genealogist. From mortality census schedules to census information, you're guaranteed to find some kind of record of any of your ancestors who ever lived in the United States. Perhaps this is why Washington, D.C. is often called, "the capitol of genealogy."

If you are able to visit the National Archives in person—something every citizen should do once in his life if only to view such grand historical documents as the Declaration of Independence, the Bill of Rights, and the Constitution, among others—you will receive a free consultation with a member of the staff, who will be able to give you much needed advice in regards to researching your family roots while inside of this palace of information.

If you can't make it to the National Archives in

person, you can do one of two things. First, you can try requesting information by mail. To do this, send a friendly, precise letter with your request to: National Archives and Records Service, NNC, Washington, D.C. 20408.

The other alternative you have if you are unable to travel to Washington, D.C., is to go to one of their regional branches, where you will find a great deal of the same information that is on file in the main branch. Here are the addresses:

For Alabama, Georgia, Florida, Kentucky, Mississippi, North Carolina, South Carolina, and Tennessee: Atlanta Federal Archives and Records Center, 1557 St. Joseph Avenue, East Point, Georgia 30344.

For Connecticut, Maine, Massachusetts, New Hampshire, Rhode Island, and Vermont: Boston Federal Archives and Records Center, 380 Trapelo Road, Waltham, Massachusetts 02154.

For Illinois, Indiana, Michigan, Minnesota, Ohio, and Wisconsin: Chicago Federal Archives and Records Center, 7358 South Pulaski Road, Chicago, Illinois 60629.

For Colorado, Montana, North Dakota, South Dakota, Utah, and Wyoming: Denver Federal Archives and Records Center, Building 48, Denver Federal Center, Denver, Colorado 80225.

For Arkansas, Louisiana, New Mexico, Oklahoma, and Texas: Fort Worth Federal Archives and Records Center, 4900 Hemphill Street, Fort

Worth, Texas 76115.

For Iowa, Kansas, Missouri, and Nebraska: Kansas City Federal Archives and Records Center, 2306 East Bannister Road, Kansas City, Missouri 64131.

For Arizona, Southern California, and Clark County, Nevada: Los Angeles Federal Archives and Records Center, 24000 Avila Road, Laguna Niguel, California 92677.

For New Jersey, New York, Puerto Rico, and Virgin Islands: New York Federal Archives and Records Center, Building 22—MOT Bayonne, Bayonne, New Jersey 07002.

For Delaware, Pennsylvania, District of Columbia, Maryland, Virginia, and West Virginia: Philadelphia Federal Archives and Records Center, 5000 Wissahickon Avenue, Philadelphia, Pennsylvania 19144.

For Northern California, Hawaii, Nevada (with the exception of Clark County), and all territories in the Pacific: San Francisco Federal Archives and Records Center, 1000 Commodore Drive, San Bruno, California 94066.

For Alaska, Idaho, Oregon, and Washington: Seattle Federal Archives and Records Center, 6125 Sand Point Way NE, Seattle, Washington 98115.

Census Records

Between the years 1600 and 1789, there were upwards of 40 censuses taken by the individual colonies and states, all of which are available for you to look at. Official censuses of the United States were first administered in 1790, and copies of the records up until the year 1910 are also available for public perusal.

United States' censuses taken from 1920 to the present are not available to the public because of the Privacy Act of 1974 which stipulated that no federal records less than 75 years old be released to the public. However, if you write to the Bureau of the Census, Pittsburg, Kansas 66762, and request a census search, they will send you a form to fill out. By sending back the completed form and a small fee, you will receive a copy of the information contained on your ancestor's census records.

Here are a few helpful hints for you to keep in mind while searching through the census files:

1) Be aware that censuses are not always accurate. The reasons for this vary, but primarily it is due to a general mistrust of census takers on the part of the public, and the occasionally deceitful census takers themselves who, because they were once paid by the number of interviews they conducted, would sometimes invent families in order to earn extra money. This shouldn't deter from utilizing the censuses, but you should try to double check the facts you gather from these records.

2) Begin with the 1910 census and work backwards, tracing your family line as far back as possible. Be sure to record all of the information available about your ancestors—whether or not it seems important at the time—onto your family and individual work sheets.

3) Be on the lookout for misspelled surnames, and always check out other families living in the same town or county as your ancestors, who also share the same last name as your ancestors. Also, just because the children in the household share the same last name with the head of the household, don't assume that they are his children. They could be nephews, servants, cousins, etc. This is especially prevalent in the earlier censuses.

Now for the censuses themselves. Listed below are the contents of all of the censuses available to the public.

1790: This census lists the names of the heads of households, the number of free white males under and over 16 years old, the number of free white females, the number of free black people, and the number of slaves. Be wary of the figures quoted for average number of family members living in the same household, as they often include people such as workers, friends, or boarders who were not actually members of the family. Also, when the British attacked Washington, D.C. during the war of 1812, the records for Delaware, Georgia, Kentucky, New Jersey, Tennessee, and Virginia were burned, although many of these lost records have been restored with the help of state tax lists.

1800, 1810: Contain the names of the heads of households, the number of free white males and females under the age of 10, and between the ages of 10 and 16, 16 and 26, 26 and 44, and over 44 years old. The census also lists the number of free black people and the number of slaves.

1820: This census lists the names of the heads of households, the number of free white males and females under 10 years old, between the ages of 10 and 16, 16 and 18, 18 and 26, 26 and 45, and over 45 years old. Also included are the number of naturalized aliens, the number of people working in the agricultural, commercial, and manufacturing industries, the number of free black people, the number of slaves, and the number of people (with the exception of Indians) who were not taxed.

1830: Contains the names of the heads of households, the number of free white people under 5 years old, 10 years old, 15 years old, 20 years old, 30 years old, 40 years old, and so on up to age 100. The census also lists the number of people working in a variety of different professions, the city, county, town, parish, district, etc., where the census was taken, the names and ages of military veterans who received pensions, the number of deaf, dumb, and insane white and black people, the number of unnaturalized aliens, and a variety of information about schools.

1840: This census lists the same information as the previous census, with the exception of number of unnaturalized citizens and information about schools.

1850, 1860: At this point, the censuses began to include a great deal more information. For every free person living in the household, there is a record of his name, address, age, sex, color, occupation (for those over 15 years old), value of real estate owned, place of birth (including the name of the state, territory, or county), marriage status, schooling, and value of personal property. For each slave, there was a record of the owner of the slave, and the slave's age, sex, and color, as well as whether the slave was a fugitive or not. Also contained were the total amount of slaves set free by every owner.

1870: This census contains the same information as the previous two, as well as a listing of blacks, Chinese, and Indians by name. Also included are the exact month of all citizens either born or married within the year.

1880: Indexed alphabetically by name, this

census records the name, age, sex, marital status and color of every person in the household, as well as their relationship to the head of the household. Additionally, the place of birth of the father and mother of the people recorded in the census is also given.

1900, 1910: The most complete censuses yet to be released, these two offer the genealogist all of the information included in the previous census, as well as the exact month and year of birth of every person living in the country.

Finally, I should mention the Mortality Census Schedules, which lists the name, age, sex, marital status, place of birth, occupation, place of death, and cause of death of all individuals who passed away during the 12 month period prior to when the census was taken. These records can be found in state libraries and through certain historical societies such as the Daughters of the American Revolution (1776 D Street, N.W., Washington, D.C.).

Military Veterans' Records

There are basically three main types of military records: the actual record of service itself, military pension applications, and land grant applications. All of these are excellent sources to utilize when trying to find information on your male ancestors.

Getting a hold of a record of your ancestor's military service is an excellent way to add some color and spice to your final product. These records often contain vivid accounts of a soldier's exploits—and who knows, you may have a bonafide war hero somewhere in your family line!

To obtain a copy of such a record, simply write to the National Archives, Washington D.C., 20408, and request a copy of GSA Form 6751. Once you complete and mail back the form, a member of the National Archives' staff will conduct a search for your ancestor's records and mail you back copies of whatever it is they find. There is usually a small photocopying fee for which you will be billed.

The types and content of the military records kept in the National Archives ranges from the Army Muster Rolls of 1784-1912 to Service files for the Bureau of Lighthouses (later known as the U.S. Coast Guard) of 1791-1929. For more information on these records, write to the National Archives at the address above, and request the "Military Service Records in the National Archives of the United States" brochure.

Probably the most important military records, however, are the pension applications. There are literally millions of such records, and the National Archives has divided them into seven categories: Revolutionary War invalid, Revolutionary War service, Old Wars, War of 1812, Mexican War, Civil War and later, and Indian Wars.

Many pension applications contain a variety of

information, including letters or affidavits from relatives, friends, and fellow soldiers, birth and marriage certificates . . . anything that would have added credence to the veteran's pension claim.

When trying to find the pension application of your ancestor, you must be able to provide the National Archives' staff with the exact state and preferably town or county that your ancestor came from. There are too many duplicate names on file for any positive identification to be made without this information.

To get a copy of your ancestor's pension application file, or to find out if one of your ancestors have ever made such a claim, write the National Archives and request GSA form 6751, just as you would do for a military record. When you receive the copy of the file, check to see if they have sent you the complete file or just one portion of it. If you feel there is more valuable information that was not sent to you, write back to the National Archives and ask them how much it will cost to obtain a copy of the complete file. They will let you know, and you can then decide if it is worth the fee—which can be fairly steep for such a request—for you to have this information.

Land grant applications are another important type of military record. These grants were one of many ways the government rewarded its veterans. Patriots (or their heirs) who fought in wars between the years 1775 and 1855, were entitled to land which was a part of the public domain. Besides providing an inducement for men to serve their country, land grants also brought about the migration of thousands of people to the wild, wild west.

Among the information contained in the land grant application files, are the veteran's name, rank, unit, term of service, age, residence, and sometimes even a physical description of said applicant. If filed by an heir, the file should include the name of the veteran, the name of the heir, their relationship, and the place and date of the veteran's death.

Land grant applications are divided into two categories: Revolutionary War and post-Revolutionary War. To obtain a copy of your ancestor's file, write to the National Archives and request that all-important GSA Form 6751.

Passenger Lists and Naturalization Records

With passenger lists, it is possible to find out when your ancestors arrived in the United States as well as what country they left from to get here. In general, the only surviving lists are from the years 1820 to 1945, and from the ports located on the Atlantic Coat or the Gulf of Mexico. The lists from the San Francisco port were destroyed by a series of fires over the years, while records from the late 18th and early 19th centuries are just plain scarce.

Passenger lists, which were filled out by the ship's captain, usually contain the name of the captain, the ship, and the port of embarkation, the name of the port, the date of the ship's arrival, and the name, age, sex, and occupation of each passenger.

Because of the many problems which confront the genealogist who is searching through passenger lists—illegible writing, gaps in the records, incomplete information and indexing—it is imperative that you know the name of the ship your ancestor came on, the name of the port of entry, and the arrival date (approximate as best you can). With this information, the staff of the National Archives just might be able to find the information you are looking for.

Naturalization records might be able to help you in your search for passenger lists, and vice-versa. In other words, if you know the name of the court where your ancestor was naturalized (this can be learned from the list of voters in the county where he lived), you can gain access to his naturalization records, which will tell you the date and the port of his arrival. Likewise, if you have enough information to get a hold of the ship's passenger list that your ancestor arrived on, you should have no problem obtaining his naturalization records.

To receive a copy of your ancestor's naturalization records, write to the Immunization and Naturalization Service, 119 D Street, N.W., Washington,

D.C. 20536 and request form N-585. After filling out and returning this form, you will be sent a file of information that should take you and your search for your family roots back to your ancestral homeland.

CHAPTER NINE

MISCELLANEOUS SOURCES

Church Records

Church records can be a secret weapon to utilize if you are having trouble locating the birth, marriage, and/or death certificates of a particular ancestor of yours. While these records vary among the different denominations, you will find that most records contain the individual's baptismal date, his place and date of birth, and the names of his parents or guardians.

Keep in mind, however, that if only one parent was a member of the church in question, then only his or her name may be listed. This is also true for the children of a married couple, who do not always join the same church as their parents, and thus would not be included on their parents' church records.

Other matters often recorded by the church include burial dates, death dates, confirmation information, and marriages and marriage banns. These latter two items usually contain the names of the bride and groom, their parents, and the witnesses. Be aware that a marriage bann is only an intention to marry, and that the couple in question may or may not have followed through with their plans.

In order to obtain the records of churches which are still in operation, you can either visit the church directly, or write to the pastor of the church. If the church records you are searching for are of a church which no longer exists, the best thing to do is to write to the archives of the particular denomination you are interested in. Here are some addresses of churches which keep archives:

American Baptist Historical Society
1100 South Goodman Street
Rochester, New York 14620

American Catholic Historical Association
Catholic University of America
Washington, D.C. 20017

Archives of the Greek Orthodox
Arch-Diocese of North America
10 East 79th Street
New York, New York 10021

Archives of the Mother Church
The First Church of Christ Scientist
107 Falmouth Street
Boston, Massachusetts 02110

Church of Jesus Christ of Latter-Day Saints
Genealogical Association
54 East South Temple St. Suite 1006
Salt Lake City, Utah 84111

Congregational Christian Historical Society
14 Beacon Street
Boston, Massachusetts 02108

Lutheran Ministerium of Pennsylvania
Historical Society
Lutheran Theological Seminary
7333 Germantown Avenue
Philadelphia, Pennsylvania 19119

Mennonite Historical Library
Bluffton College
Bluffton, Oho 45817

Moravian Archives
North Main at Elizabeth
Bethlehem, Pennsylvania 18015

Presbyterian & Reformed Church
Historical Foundation
Assembly Drive
Montreat, North Carolina 28757

The Protestant Episcopal Church
Church Historical Society
606 Rathervue Place
Austin, Texas 78700

Searching Graveyards

If you are having trouble finding church or
government records regarding the death of one
of your ancestors, your next step might be to visit
the graveyard where your ancestor is buried. In
fact, you may want to do this in order to find out a
variety of information, from names and dates of
death of other family members who may be
buried in the same cemetery or family plot, to
occupations, heritage, and other insightful information which may be written on the gravestone
itself.

To locate the cemetery your ancestor is buried in,
contact a local historical society in the town which

your ancestor died, or simply contact local cemeteries in the town and county where you think your ancestor may be buried. If you would like to photograph your ancestor's gravestone, make sure you bring along a shovel, a small pair of shears, a wire brush, and some chalk with you when you visit the grave site. After clearing away and cleaning up the area around the headstone and the stone itself, rub the piece of chalk over the gravestone so that the lettering will be easy to read in your photograph.

When you copy down information that is printed on the headstone, make sure you write down everything that appears in the exact manner which it is written on the stone itself. Older gravestones are often written in an archaic or foreign language, and by writing everything down precisely as it appears on the gravestone, you will make it much easier on yourself when it comes time to translate the information.

Schools, Colleges and Fraternity Records

Educational files often contain a great deal of biographical data which can be of immense use to the genealogist. If you know precisely where your ancestor lived, you can check local records to find out which schools were in existence at that time and then try to seek out the records of these schools. Beginning with the private school of your ancestor's religious affiliation may save you time, since this was how many private schools operated before the existence of a public school system.

If you think that your ancestor may have attended college, you might want to check with some of the older universities around the country, including: William Penn in Philadelphia, Boston Latin School, Harvard, William and Mary, Roxbury Latin School in Roxbury, Massachusetts, and Yale. These institutions of higher education have enrollment records, yearbooks, rosters, and student files reaching all the back to their founding years.

Finally, contacting the National Interfraternity Conference through a local university may ultimately lead you to a great deal of biographical information on one of your ancestors if, of course, he was a member of a fraternity at one time or another.

Newspapers

Newspapers have existed since before the United States was an independent country. While searching through microfilms of newspapers can be quite a chore, the proliferation of newspaper indexes within the last few years has made this research process much less time consuming.

The most obvious information contained in newspapers that is useful to the genealogist are marriage and birth notices, and obituaries. However, papers such as the *Boston Evening Transcript* have published a genealogical column aimed specifically at people who are searching for lost relatives and information on ancestors who have long since passed away. Check with your local library or, visit or write to the Library of Congress and ask for information on newspaper indexes and how to utilize them best.

Private Clubs

The last type of miscellaneous records I will discuss are those kept by the private clubs which have existed in this country for decades and decades. The Elks, Masons, Knights of Columbus, and the Rotary, Kiwanis, and Lions clubs have files on their members dating back to the founders of the association.

Such records contain highly detailed biographical information and occasionally even photographs of the member. You should contact the local president of the club—either in your or your ancestor's home town—that you believe your ancestor may have belonged to in order to find out how you can receive a copy of your ancestor's file.

CHAPTER TEN

GENEALOGICAL/ HISTORICAL SOCIETIES AND THEIR PUBLICATIONS

Joining a Genealogical/Historical Society

By joining a genealogical/historical society, you gain access to magazines, books, libraries . . . a host of genealogical information that can only save you time and money, while providing you with facts you may have never thought would be possible to discover. The Genealogy Club of America is an excellent society for the beginning genealogist to hook up with, as they tend to take a more serious view of people who are simply interested in tracing their family roots as opposed to other societies who are primarily concerned with professional genealogists.

Listed below are the names and addresses of genealogical/historical societies from across the country. Since the membership rules (some require no membership at all in order to use their facilities while others are more rigid) and resource materials vary from organization to organization, I suggest you begin with those societies closest to your home or the home of the ancestor you are most interested in researching.

ALABAMA

Alabama Genealogical Society
Box 35
Epea, AL 35460

Birmingham Genealogical Society
Box 2432
Birmingham, AL 35201

East Alabama Genealogical Society
c/o Mrs. J. H. Strothan
Box 484
Dadeville, AL 36853

Mobile Genealogical Society
Box 6224
Mobile, AL 36606

ALASKA

Anchorage Genealogy Society
Box 100412
Anchorage, AK 99510

ARIZONA

Arizona Society of Genealogists
6565 E. Grant Road
Tucson, AZ 85715

Arizona State Genealogical Society
Box 42075
Tucson, AZ 85733-2075

ARKANSAS

Ark-La-Tex Genealogical Assn., Inc.
P.O. Box 4462
Shreveport, LA 71104

Arkansas Genealogical Society
4200 A St.
Little Rock, AR 72205

Madison County Genealogical Society
P.O. Box 427
Huntsville, AR 72740

Northeast Arkansas Genealogical Association
314 Vine St.
Newport, AR 73112

Northwest Arkansas Genealogical Society
P.O. Box K
Rogers, AR 72756

CALIFORNIA

California Central Coast Genealogical Society
Box 4
Atascadero, CA 93423-0004

California Genealogical Society
2099 Pacific Ave.
San Francisco, CA 94115

Contra Costa County Genealogical Society
Box 910
Concord, CA 94522

Fresno Genealogical Society
Box 1429
Fresno, CA 93716

Genealogical Society of Riverside
Box 2664
Riverside, CA 92506

Genealogical Society of Santa Cruz County
Box 72
Santa Cruz, CA 95060

Hi Desert Genealogical Society
Box 616
Victorville, CA 92392

Kern County Genealogical Society
Box 2214
Bakersfield, CA 93303

The Mojave Desert Genealogical Society
Box 1320
Barstow, CA 92311

Orange County Genealogical Society
Box 1587
Orange, CA 92668

Paradise Genealogical Society
Box 460
Paradise, CA 95969-0460

Redwood Genealogical Society
Box 645
Fortuna, CA 95540

San Bernardino Valley Genealogical Society
Box 2505
San Bernardino, CA 92406

San Diego Genealogical Society
3030 Kellogg St.
San Diego, CA 92106

Southern California Genealogical Society
103 S. Golden Mall
Burbank, CA 91502

Sutter-Yuba Genealogical Society
Box 1274
Yuba City, CA 95991

COLORADO

Boulder Genealogical Society
Box 3246
Boulder, CO 80303

Colorado Genealogical Society
P.O. Box 9671
Denver, CO 80209

Larimer County Genealogical Society
600 S. Shields
Fort Collins, CO 80521

CONNECTICUT

Connecticut Society of Genealogists, Inc.
P.O. Box 435
Glastonburg, CT 06033

Descendents of the Illegitimate Sons and
   Daughters of the Kings of Britain
c/o Brainer T. Peck
Lakeside, CT 06758

Stamford Genealogical Society
Box 249
Stamford, CT 06904

DELAWARE

Delaware Genealogical Society
505 Market Street Mall
Wilmington, DE 19801

DISTRICT OF COLUMBIA

National Genealogical Society
1921 Sunderland Pl., N.W.
Washington, D.C. 20036

National Society of the Children of the American
  Revolution
1776 D Street N.W.
Washington, D.C. 20006

National Society of the Colonial Dames of the
  XVII Century
1300 New Hampshire Avenue, N.W.
Washington, D.C. 20036

National Society of the Daughters of the
  American Revolution
1776 D Street N.W.
Washington, D.C. 20006

National Society of the Daughters of the
  Founders and Patriots of America
1307 New Hampshire Avenue, N.W.
Washington, D.C. 20036

National Society of the Sons of the American
  Revolution
2412 Massachusetts Avenue, N.W.
Washington, D.C. 20008

National Society of Women Descendents of the
  Ancient and Honorable Artillery Company
3627 Chesapeake Street, N.W.
Washington, D.C. 20008

Society of the Cincinnati
2118 Massachusetts Avenue, N.W.
Washington, D.C. 20008

FLORIDA

Florida Genealogical Society
Box 18624
Tampa, FL 33609

Manasota Genealogical Society, Inc.
Box 9433
Bradenton, FL 33506

Palm Beach County Genealogical Society
Box 1745
W. Palm Beach, FL 33402

Polk County Genealogical Society
Box 1719
Bartow, FL 33830

Southern Genealogist's Exchange Society
Box 2801
Jacksonville, FL 32203

GEORGIA

Georgia Genealogical Society
Box 38066
Atlanta, GA 30334

IDAHO

Idaho Genealogical Society
325 State St.
Boise, ID 83702

ILLINOIS

Bloomington-Normal Genealogical Society
Box 488
Normal, IL 61761

Chicago Genealogical Society
Box 1160
Chicago, IL 60690

Cumberland and Coles County Genealogical
   Society
Rt. 1, Box 141
Toledo, IL 62468

Decatur Genealogical Society
Box 2205
Decatur, IL 62526

Genealogical Society of Southern Illinois
c/o Logan College
Carterville, IL 62818

Great River Genealogical Society
c/o Quincy Public Library
Quincy, IL 62302

Illiana Genealogical Society
Box 207
Danville, IL 61834

Iroquois County Genealogical Society
Old Courthouse Museum
103 W. Cherry St.
Watseka, IL 60970

Knox County Genealogical Society
Box 13
Galesburg, IL 61401

Lexington Genealogical Society
304 N. Elm St.
Lexington, IL 61753

Moultrie County Genealogical Society
Box MM
Sullivan, IL 61951

National Woman's Relief Coprs (Auxiliary to the
  Grand Army of the Republic)
629 South Seventh
Springfield, IL 62703

Peoria Genealogical Society
Box 1489
Peoria, IL 61655

Sangamon County Genealogical Society
Box 1829
Springfield, IL 62705

INDIANA

Elkhart County Genealogical Society
Rt. 5, Box 48
Elkhart, IN 46514

Genealogical Section of the Indiana Historical
  Society
140 N. Senate Ave.
Indianapolis, IN 46204

Pulaski County Genealogical Society
RR 1
Winamac, IL 46996

IOWA

Iowa Genealogical Society
Box 3815
Des Moines, IA 50322

Lee County Genealogical Society
Box 303
Keokuk, IA 52632

KANSAS

Finney County Genealogical Society
P.O. Box 592
Garden City, KS 67846

Fort Hayes Kansas College Library
Hays, KS 67601

Heritage Genealogical Society
W.A. Rankin Memorial Library
Neodeska, KS 66757

Johnson County Genealogical Society
P.O. Box 8057
Shawnee Mission, KS 66208

Kansas Genealogical Society
Box 103
Dodge City, KS 67801

Montgomery County Genealogical Society
Box 444
Coffeyville, KS 67337

Riley County Genealogical Society
2005 Claflin Road
Manhattan, KS 66502

Thomas County Genealogical Society
375 W. 4th
Colby, KS 67701

Topeka Genealogical Society
P.O. Box 4048
Topeka, KS 66604

KENTUCKY

Central Kentucky Genealogical Society
Box 153
Frankfort, KY 40601

West-Central Kentucky Family Research
  Association
Box 1465
Owensboro, KY 42301

LOUISIANA

Genealogical Association
Box 71
Shreveport, LA 71161

Genealogical Research Society of New Orleans
Box 51791
New Orleans, LA 70150

Louisiana Genealogical Society
Box 3454
Baton Rouge, LA 70821

MARYLAND

Maryland Genealogical Society
201 West Monument St.
Baltimore, MD 21201

Prince George's County Genealogical Society
Box 819
Bowie, MD 20715

Unitarian and Universalist Genealogical Society
3608 Clifmar Road
Baltimore, MD 21207

MASSACHUSETTS

New England Historic and Genealogical Society
101 Newberry St.
Boston, MA 02116

Pilgrim Society
Pilgrim Hall Museum
Plymouth, MA 02360

MICHIGAN

Detroit Society for Genealogical Research
Detoit Public Library
5201 Woodward Ave.
Detroit, MI 48202

Flint Genealogical Society
P.O. Box 1217
Flint, MI 48501

Kalamazoo Valley Genealogical Society
315 Rose St.
Kalamazoo, MI 49006

Mid-Michigan Genealogical Society
3800 Glasgow Dr.,
Lansing, MI 48910

Muskegon County Genealogical Society
Hackley Library
316 W. Webster Ave.
Muskegon, MI 49440

Saginaw Genealogical Society
c/o Saginaw Public Library
505 Janes Ave.
Saginaw, MI 48607

Western Michigan Genealogical Society
Grand Rapids Public Library
Grand Rapids, MI 49503

MINNESOTA

Anoka County Genealogical Society
1900 3rd Ave.
Anoka, MN 55303

Ladies of the Grand Army of the Republic
3515 East Minnehaha Parkway
Minneapolis, MN 55417

Minnesota Genealogical Society
P.O. Box 16069
St. Paul, MN 55116

Range Genealogical Society
Box 278
Buhl, MN 55713

MISSISSIPPI

The Heart of America Genealogical Society
c/o Missouri Valley Rm.
Kansas City Public Library
311 E. 21st St.
Kansas City, MO 64106

Ozarks Genealogical Society
Box 3494
Springfield, MO 65804

St. Louis Genealogical Society
1695 S. Brentwood Blvd.
Suite 203
St. Louis, MO 63144

West Central Missouri Genealogical Society
705 Broad St.
Warrensburg, MO 64093

NEBRASKA

Fort Kearny Genealogical Society
Box 22
Kearny, NE 68847

Madison County Genealogical Society
Box 347
Norfolk, NE 68701

North Platte Genealogical Society
c/o North Platte Library
4th and Vine
North Platte, NE 69101

NEW HAMPSHIRE

New Hampshire Society of Genealogists
Strafford County Chapter
P.O. Box 322
Dover, NH 03820

NEW JERSEY

Genealogical Society of New Jersey
P.O. Box 1291
New Brunswick, NJ 08903

Hereditary Order of Descendents of Colonial
   Governors
"Pinecroft"
Harter Road
Morristown, NJ

National Society of the Colonial Daughters of the
   17th Century
51 King's Highway W.
Haddonfield, NJ 08033

NEW MEXICO

New Mexico Genealogical Society
Box 8330
Albuquerque, NM 87108-8330

NEW YORK

Central New York Genealogical Society
Box 104
Colvin Stn.
Syracuse, NY 13205

Colonial Dames of America
421 East 61st Street
New York, NY 10021

Daughters of the Cincinnati
122 East 58th Street
New York, NY 10022

Genealogical Society of Colonial Wars
600 Third Avenue
New York, NY 10016

General Society of the Sons of the Revolution
Fraunces Tavern
54 Pearl Street
New York, NY 10004

National Society of Colonial Dames of America
215 East 71st Street
New York, NY 10021

National Society of New England Women
69 Kensington Road
Bronxville, NY 10708

New York Genealogical and Biographical Society
122 East 58th Street
New York, NY 10022

Order of Colonial Lords of Manors in America
c/o Robert D.L. Gardiner
230 Park Avenue
New York, NY 10017

Order of the Founders and Patriots of America
c/o Federal Hall Memorial
15 Pine Street
New York, NY 10005

St. Nicholas Society of the City of New York
122 East 58th Street
New York, NY 10022

Twin Tiers Genealogical Society
230 Devonshire Dr.
Elmire, NY 14903

Ulster County Genealogical Society
P.O. Box 333
Hurley, NY 11443

NORTH CAROLINA

Genealogical Society of the Original Wilkes
  County
Wilkesboro, NC 28659

North Carolina Genealogical Society
Box 1492
Raleigh, NC 27602

Wilkes Genealogical Society, Inc.
Box 1629
North Wilkesboro, NC 28659

NORTH DAKOTA

Bismarck-Mandan Genealogical Society
Box 485
Bismarck, ND 58501

Mouse River Loop Genealogy Society
Box 1391
Minot, ND 58701

OHIO

Ashtabula County Genealogical Society
Henderson Library
54 E. Jefferson St.
Jefferson, OH 44047

Lake County Genealogical Society
Morley Public Library
184 Phelps St.
Parinsville, OH 44077

Miami Valley Genealogical Society
Box 1364
Dayton, OH 45401

Northwestern Ohio Genealogical Society
P.O. Box 17066
Toledo, OH 43615

Ohio Genealogical Society
419 W. 3rd St.
Mansfield, OH 44906

Ohio Genealogical Society
P.O. Box 2625
Ashland, OH 44906

West August Genealogical Society
1510 Prairie Dr.
Belpre, OH 45714

OKLAHOMA

National Society of the United States Daughters
  of 1812
c/o Mrs. Ira J. Dietrich
1421 E. 19th Street
Tulsa, OK 74120

Oklahoma Genealogical Society
Box 314
Oklahoma City, OK 73101

Tulsa Genealogical Society
Box 585
Tulsa, OK 74101

OREGON

Coos Bay Genealogical Forum
Box 1211
Coos Bay, OR 97420

Genealogical Forum of Portland
1410 S.W. Morrison, Rm. 812
Portland, OR 97205

Mt. Hood Genealogical Forum
Box 208
Oregon City, OR 97045

Oregon Genealogical Society
P.O. Box 1214
Eugene, OR 97400

Rogue Valley Genealogical Society
125 S. Central Ave.
Medford, OR 97501

Williamette Valley Genealogical Society
Box 2083
Salem, OR 97308

PENNSYLVANIA

Dames of the Loyal Legion of the United States
4237 Sansom Street
Philadelphia, PA 19104

Descendents of the Signers of the Declaration of
    Independence
c/o Historical Society of Pennsylvania
1300 Locust Street
Philadelphia, PA 19107

Erie Society for Genealogical Research
Box 1403
Erie, PA 16512

Genealogical Society of Pennsylvania
1300 Locust Street
Philadelphia, PA 19107

General Society of the War of 1812
3311 Columbia Pike
Lancaster, PA 17603

Military Order of the Loyal Legion of the United
  States
1805 Pine Street
Philadelphia, PA 19103

Pennsylvania German Society
R.D. 1
Breinigsville, PA 18031

Scotch-Irish Society of the United States of
  America
2301 Packard Building
Philadelphia, PA 19102

Society of the War of 1812 in the Commonwealth
  of Pennsylvania
c/o Russel Bement, Jr.
108 Avon Road
Haverford, PA 19041

Society of the Whiskey Rebellion of 1794
Dallowgill
3311 Columbia Pike
Lancaster, PA 17603

Sons and Daughters of Pioneer Rivermen
121 River Avenue
Sewickley, PA 15143

Sons of Union Veterans of the Civil War
Post Office Box 24
Gettysburg, PA 17325

Sons of Union Veterans of the Civil War Auxiliary
5137 North Howard Street
Philadelphia, PA

Somerset Genealogical Society
Box 533
Somerset, PA 15501

RHODE ISLAND

Rhode Island Genealogical Society
P.O. Box 7618
Warwick RI 02887-7618

SOUTH CAROLINA

South Carolina Genealogical Association
P.O. Box 1442
Lexington, SC 29072

SOUTH DAKOTA

Rapid City Society for Genealogical Research
Box 1495
Rapid City, SD 57701

TENNESSEE

Mid-West Tennessee Genealogical Society
Box 3343
Jackson, TN 38301

Tennessee Genealogical Society
Box 12124
Memphis, TN 38112

Watauga Association of Genealogists
Sherrod Library, Rm. 301
East Tennessee State University
Johnson City, TN 37601

TEXAS

Amarillo Genealogical Society
Amarillo Public Library
300 E. 4th
Amarillo, TX 79189

Austin Genealogical Society
Box 774
Austin, TX 78767

Central Texas Genealogical Society
1717 Austin Ave.
Waco, TX 76701

Chaparral Genealogical Society
Box 606
Tomball, TX 77375

Daughters of the Republic of Texas
Old Land Office Building
11th and Brazos Street
Austin, TX 78701

Fort Worth Genealogical Society
Box 9767
Ft. Worth, TX 76107

Hispanic Genealogical Society
P.O. Box 55186
Houston, TX 77055

Hood's Texas Brigade Association
Confederate Research Center
Post Office Box 619
Hillsboro, TX 76645

McLennan County Society
1717 Austin Ave.
Waco, TX 76701

National Society of the Sons and Daughters of
 the Pilgrims
2714 Green Avenue
Fort Worth, TX 76109

Mesquite Genealogical Society
Box 165
Mesquite, TX 75149

Midland Genealogical Society
Box 1191
Midland, TX 79702

San Angelo Genealogical Society
Box 3453
San Angelo, TX 76901

San Antonio Genealogical Society
Box 5907
San Antonio, TX 78201-0907

Southeast Texas Genealogical Society
c/o Tyrrel Historical Library
P.O. Box 3827
Beaumont, TX 77704

Texas State Genealogical Society
c/o Mrs. Joe B. Golden
2100 Hartford
Austin, TX 78703

Tip O'Texas Genealogical Society
Harlingen Public Library
Harlingen, TX 78550

UTAH

Genealogy Club of America
420 S. 425 West
Bountiful, UT 84010

National Society of the Daughters of Utah
  Pioneers
300 North Main
Salt Lake City, UT 84103

National Society of the Sons of Utah Pioneers
2998 Connor Street (2150 East)
Salt Lake City, UT 84109

Utah County Genealogical Society
110 S. 300 W.
Provo, UT 84601

Utah Genealogical Association
Box 1144
Salt Lake City, UT 84110

VERMONT

Genealogical Society of Vermont
Westminster West, RFD 3
Putney, VT 05346

Vermont Genealogical Society
P.O. Box 422
Pittsford, VT 05763

VIRGINIA

American Society of Genealogists
2255 Cedar Ln.
Vienna, VA 22180

Children of the Confederacy
328 North Boulevard
Richmond, VA 23220

Genealogical Society of Tidewater
Thomas Nelson Community College
P.O. Box 9407
Hampton, VA 23670

Jamestowne Society
4313 North Ashlawn Drive
Richmond, VA 23221

United Daughters of the Confederacy
328 North Boulevard
Richmond, VA 23220

WASHINGTON

Eastern Washington Genealogical Society
Box 1826
Spokane, WA 99210

Lower Columbia Genealogical Society
Box 472
Longview, WA 98632

Olympia Genealogical Society
Olympia Public Library
8th and Franklin
Olympia, WA 98501

Seattle Genealogical Society
Box 549
Seattle, WA 98111

The Tacoma Genealogical Society
Box 1952
Tacoma, WA 98401

Tri-City Genealogical Society
Route 1, Box 5006
Richland, WA 99352

Whatcom County Washington Genealogical
  Society
P.O. Box 1493
Bellingham, WA 98227-1493

Yakima Valley Genealogical Society
Box 445
Yakima, WA 98907

WEST VIRGINIA

Marion County Genealogical Club, Inc.
Marion County Library
Monroe St.
Fairmont, WV 26554

Wetzel County Genealogical Society
Box 464
New Martinsville, WV 26155

WISCONSIN

Milwaukee County Genealogical Society
916 E. Lyon St.
Milwaukee, WI 53202

Wisconsin State Genealogical Society
c/o Mrs. John M. Irwin
2109 20th Ave.
Monroe, WI 53566

WYOMING

Cheyenne Genealogical Society
Laramie County Library
Central Ave.
Cheyenne, WY 82001

Genealogical Periodicals

Genealogical periodicals have been published throughout the history of the United States which, of course, means that there is an overwhelming amount of published material out there to sort through. Fortunately, there exists a good number of indexes to these publications, which can make locating a particular article or piece of valuable information about one of your ancestors relatively easy. Here are the names of the more informative indexes:

Barber, Gertrude A., comp. *Subject Index of the New York Genealogical and Biographical Record, Volumes 39-76 Inclusive.* New York: The Author, 1946.

Brigham, Clarence S. *History and Bibliography of American Newspapers, 1690-1820.* 2 vols. Worcester, Mass.: 1947.

Cappon, Lester J. *American Genealogical Periodicals: A Bibliography with a Chronological Finding-List.* New York: New York Public Library, 1962.

Columbia Library Club, comp. *The Missouri Historical Index: Volumes 1-25.* Columbia: The State Historical Society of Missouri, 1934.

Cruise, Boyd, comp. *Index to the Louisiana Historical Quarterly.* New Orleans: Plantation Bookshop, 1956.

Daughters of the American Revolution. *Genealogical Guide. Master Index of Genealogy in the DAR Magazine, vols. 184, 1892-1950.* Washington, D.C.: Daughters of the American Revolution, 1951.

Doll, Eugene E., ed. *The Pennsylvania Magazine of History and Biography: Index, Volumes 1-75.* Philadelphia: The Historical Society of Pennsylvania, 1954.

Everton, George B., ed. *The Handy Book for Genealogists.* Logan, Utah: Everton Publishers, 1971.

Fisher, Carlton E. *Topical Index, Vols. 1-50, 1912-1962.* National Genealogical Society, special pub. 29. Washington, D.C.: The Society, 1964.

Genealogical Periodical Annual Index, Vols. 1— 1962—. Bladensburg, Md.: Ellen S. Rogers. Bowie, Md.: George E. Russell.

Gerould, Winifred. American Newspapers, 1821-*1936. A Union List of Files Available in the United States and Canada.* New York: 1937.

Gregory, James P., Jr., comp. *Missouri Historical Review: Cumulative Index to Volumes 26-45.* Columbia: The State Historical Society of Missouri, 1955.

Index to the Wisconsin Magazine of History, Volumes 26-35. Madison: The State Historical Society of Wisconsin, 1955.

Jacobus, Donald L. *Index to Genealogical Periodicals.* Vol. 1, 1858-1931; vol. 2, 1932-1946; vol. 3, 1947-1952. Reprint. Baltimore: Genealogical Publishing Co., 1963-65.

Krueger, Lillian, comp. *The Wisconsin Magazine of History: Index, Volumes 1-15.* Madison: The State Historical Society of Wisconsin, 1934.

Parsons, Margaret Wellington, ed. *Index (Abridged) to the New England Historical and Genealogical Register: Volumes 51 through 112.* Marlborough, Massachusetts: The Author, 1959.

Riker, Dorothy, comp. *Indiana Magazine of History: General Index, Volumes 1-25.* 1930. Reprint. New York: Kraus Reprint Corp., 1967.

Royne, Josephine E., and Chapman, Effie L., eds. *New England Historical and Genealogical Register: Index of Persons, Subjects, Places, Vols. 1-50.* 3 vols 1906-1911. Reprint. Baltimore: GPC, 1972.

Russell, George E. Genealogical Periodicals Annual Index. Vol. 5—, 1966—. Bowie, Md.: The Author, 1967—.

Spear, Dorothea N. *Bibliography of American Directories Through 1860.* Worcester, Massachusetts: American Antiquarian Society, 1961.

Supplement to Genealogical Guide: Master Index of Genealogy in the DAR Magazine, Vols. 85-89, 1950-1955. Washington, D.C.: Daughters of the American Revolustion, 1956.

Swem, E.G., comp. *Virginia Historical Index.* Gloucester, Mass.: Peter Smith, 1965.

Waldenmaier, Inez. *Annual Index to Genealogical Periodicals and Family Histories.* Vols. for 1956-1962. Washington, D.C.

Youngs, Florence E. *Subject Index of the New York Genealogical & Biographical Record, Vols. 1-38.* New York, 1907.

Where to Buy Genealogical Publications

Whether you locate a particular publication in one of the indexes mentioned above, or if you just simply want to inquire about published material on a certain region of the country, the following genealogical publishers and book sellers should be able to help you. Write to them requesting either their catalog (usually free) or information on a particular publication that you are interested in.

EAST

Carl-Del-Scribe
Box 746
Burlington, VT 05401

Connecticut Society of Genealogists, Inc.
Box 305
West Hartford, CT 06107

Genealogist's Bookshelf
Box 468, 330 E. 85th St.
New York, NY 10028

Hoenstine Book Mart
Box 208
Holidaysburg, PA 16648

George S. MacManus Company
2022 Walnut St.
Philadelphia, PA 19103

New England Historic and Genealogical Society
101 Newbury St.
Boston, MA 02116

New York Public Library
Grand Central Station, Box 2747
New York, NY 10017

Charles E. Tuttle Company, Inc.
Rutland, VT 05701

SOUTH

American Association for State and Local
  History
132 9th Ave. North
Nashville, TN 37208

Boarderland Books
Anchorage, KY

Genealogical Book Company
521-23 St. Paul's Pl.
Baltimore, MD 21202

Genealogical Publishing Company
521-523 St. Paul's Pl.
Baltimore, MD 21202

Holmes-Corey Antiquities
Box 115 M
Marco Island, FL 33937

Kentucky Publishing Company
153 Cherokee Park
Lexington, KY 40503

Magna Carta Book Company
5324 Beaufort Ave.
Baltimore, MD 21215

Polyanthos, Inc.
833 Orleans St.
New Orleans, LA 70116

Reprint Company
154 W. Cleveland Park Dr.
Spartanburg, SC 29303

Southern Historical Press
Box 229
Easley, SC 29640

Walton-Folk Americana
330 Cherokee St.
Kennesaw, GA 30144

MIDWEST

Bland Books
401 N.W. 10th St.
Fairfield, IL 62837

The Bookmark
Box 74
Knightstown, IN 46148

Gale Research Company
Book Tower
Detroit, MI 48226

Heritage Resource Center
Box 26305
Minneapolis, MN 55426

Hoosier Heritage Press
520 N. Campbell St.
Indianapolis, IN 46219

WEST

Ancient Book Shop
Box 986
Santa Fe, NM

The Augustan Society
Hartwell Company
1617 W. 261st St.
Harbor City, CA 90710

Brigham Young University Press
205 University Press Bldg.
Provo, UT 84602

Dawson Book Shop
550 S. Figueroa St.
Los Angeles, CA 90017

Deseret Book Company
44 E. South Temple
Salt Lake City, UT 84110

Everton Publishers, Inc.
Box 368
Logan, UT 84321

Hawkes Publishing, Inc.
156 W. 2170 South
Salt Lake City, UT 84115

Heritage Research Institute
964 Laird Ave.
Salt Lake City, UT 84105
(Origins of names)

Saddleback Book Shop
Box 10393
Santa Ana, CA 92771

San Francisco Historical Records
1204 Nimitz Dr.
Colma, CA 94015

CHAPTER ELEVEN

BRINGING YOUR NEW, EXTENDED FAMILY TOGETHER

Why Unite Your Extended Family?

Bringing together your extended family should be looked upon as the ultimate goal of your search for your family roots. In today's hectic age, when so many of our country's traditional values seem to be falling by the wayside, keeping a strong sense of your family's heritage is more important than ever. Children in particular relish the comfort and security that comes along with a sense of family history, of generation succeeding generation, and of carrying on the honor and tradition of the family name.

How to Arrange an Extended Family Gathering

The best way to go about getting together your newfound family is to plan a reunion over a holiday weekend. Pick a location in a region of the country that is somewhat central to where the majority of your family members live. If possible, try to choose a spot that is in some way relevant to the history of your family—perhaps the city where one of the family's oldest ancestors lived.

You should have plenty of copies of the material you have collected during your search available for everyone to see, including family and individual work sheets, photographs, newspaper clippings, diaries, birth, marriage and death certificates and the like. It is also a good idea to bring along a tape recorder and either a still camera or a video camera so that you will be able to record the events that take place over the weekend, including all of the valuable stories that will surely be told by family members about their ancestors.

CHAPTER TWELVE

SEARCHING FOR YOUR ANCESTRAL HOMELAND

Begin at Home

Any search for your ancestral homeland should begin right here in the United States. Before spending the money, time and energy that goes into either writing or traveling overseas, you should gather all the information you can about the ancestors of those countries you will be researching.

To begin with, you will at least need to know the name of your ancestor, the country and city where he came from, and the approximate date of his immigration. The next step would be to contact the LDS library in Salt Lake City, or one of their regional branches in your area, to see what kind of information they have about your ancestor on their files. You'll be pleasantly surprised to know that, along with their vast collection of American genealogical records, the LDS library has a sizable amount of information on countries who have supplied the United States with immigrants.

The staff at the LDS library will also provide you with the addresses of foreign agencies who may be able to supply you with the records of birth, death, marriage, etc. which you will ultimately be searching for. If, for some reason, the LDS library does not have the addresses for the particular country you are interested in, or if the agencies overseas prove to be of no help, try writing to the American embassy in the country or city you are interested in researching and ask them if they can be of any assistance.

In general, you should conduct all of your foreign correspondence just as you would do in the United States; after all, most countries have the same type of record keeping system as we do, with census data, military information, tax records, etc. all readily available. Always remember to include enough international reply coupons to cover the cost of having your overseas connection answer any of your inquiries.

While searching for your family roots in foreign countries is a highly challenging and often—in the case of Iron Curtain countries—frustrating experience, the rewards of such a search defy description. To be able to walk on the same ground that your ancestor stepped on hundreds of years ago, to correspond with a distant relative in a far away country, to discover that your ancestor was a famous artist or writer whose works you've always admired but whom you never dreamed you were related to . . . these experiences are like no other, as they link you to other worlds and other lifetimes that you perhaps never even knew existed but are actually as much a part of you as the small town or neighborhood that you grew up in.

CHAPTER THIRTEEN

STATE-BY-STATE REFERENCE LIST

ALABAMA

Bureau of Vital Statistics
State Department of Public Health
Montgomery, Al 36104

Institute of Genealogical and Historical Research
Samford University Library
800 Lakeshore Dr.
Birmingham, AL 35208

ALASKA

Bureau of Vital Statistics
Department of Health and Welfare
Pounch "H"
Juneau, AK 99801

Alaska Historical Library
Pounch "G"
State Capitol
Juneau, AK 99801

ARIZONA

Division of Vital Statistics
State Department of Health
P.O. Box 6820
Phoenix, AZ 85005

Arizona State Department of Library and Archives
Third Floor
State Capitol
Phoenix, AZ 85007

ARKANSAS

Bureau of Vital Statistics
State Department of Health
Little Rock, AR 72201

Arkansas History Commission
Old State House
Little Rock, AR 72201

CALIFORNIA

Bureau of Vital Statistics
State Department of Public Health
1927 Thirteenth Street
Sacramento, CA 95814

California Historical Society
2090 Jackson Street
San Francisco, CA 94109

California State Archives
R. 200, 1020 "O" St.
Sacramento, CA 95814

Conference of California Historical Societies
Univesity of Pacific
Stockton, California 95204

Genealogical Research Center
Department of Special Collections
San Francisco Public Library
Civic Center
San Francisco, CA 94102

COLORADO

Records and Statistics Section
Colorado Department of Health
4210 East Eleventh Avenue
Denver, CO 80220

Records and Statistics Section
Colorado Department of Health
4210 East Eleventh Avenue
Denver, CO 80203

CONNECTICUT

Public Health Statistics Section
State Department of Health
79 Elm street
Hartford, CT 06115

Connecticut Historical Society and Library
1 Elizabeth Street
Hartford, CT 06105

Connecticut League of Historical Studies
114 Whitney Avenue
New Haven, CT 06510

DELAWARE

Bureau of Vital Statistics
State Board of Health
State Health Building
Dover, DE 19901

Historical Society of Delaware
Sixth and Market Streets
Wilmington, DE 19801

Public Archives Commission
Hall of Records
Dover, DE 19901

FLORIDA

Bureau of Vital Statistics
State Board of Health
P.O. Box 210
Jacksonville, FL 32201

Florida Board of Archives and History
401 East Gaines Street
Tallahassee, Fl 32301

Florida Historical Studies
University of South Florida Library
Tampa, FL 33620

GEORGIA

Vital Records SDervice
State Department of Public Health
47 Trinity Avenue, S.W.
Atlanta, GA 30334

Georgia Department of Archives and History
330 Capital Avenue, S.E.
Atlanta, GA 30334

Georgia Historical Commission
116 Mitchell Street, S.W.
Atlanta, GA 30303

HAWAII

Research and Statistics Office
State Department of Health
P.O. Box 3378
Honolulu, HI 96801

DAR Memorial Library
1914 Makiki Hts. Dr.
Honolulu, HI 96822

Hawaiian Historical Society
560 Kawaiahao Street
Honolulu, HI 96803

Public Archives Library
Iolani Palace Grounds
Honolulu, HI 96813

IDAHO

Bureau of Vital Statistics
State Department of Health
Boise, ID 83701

Idaho State Historical Society and Library
610 North Julia Davis Drive
Boise, ID 83706

ILLINOIS

Bureau of Statistics
State Department of Public Health
Springfield, IL 62706

Illinois State Archives
Archives Bldg.
Springfield, IL 62706

Illinois State Historical Society and Library
Centennial Building
Springfield, IL 62706

INDIANA

Division of Vital Records
State Board of Health
1330 West Michigan Street

Division of Vital Records
State Board of Health
1330 West Michigan Street
Indianapolis, IN 46206

Indiana Historical Bureau
State Library and Historical Building
Indianapolis, IN 46204

Indiana Historical Society and Library
140 North Senate Avenue
Indianapolis, IN 46204

IOWA

Division of Records and Statistics
State Department of Health
Des Moines, IA 50319

State Historical Society of Iowa Library
University of Iowa
Iowa City, IA 52240

KANSAS

Division of Vital Statistics
State Department of Health
Topeka, KS 66612

Kansas State Historical Society and Library
120 West Tenth Street
Topeka, KS 66612

KENTUCKY

Office of Vital Statistics
State Department of Health
275 East Main Street
Frankfort, KY 40601

Kentucky Historical Society
Old State House
P.O. Box H
Frankfort, KY 40601

LOUISIANA

Division of Public Health Statistics
State Board of Health
P.O. Box 60630
New Orleans, LA 70160
Bureau of Vital Statistics
City Health Department
1W03 City Hall, Civic Center
New Orleans, LA 70112

Howard Tilton Library
Map and Genealogy Rm.
Tulane University
New Orleans, LA 70118

Louisiana Historical Association
Box 44222—Capital Station
Baton Rouge, LA 70804

MAINE

Office of Vital Statistics
State Department of Health and Welfare
State House
Augusta, ME 04330

Maine Historical Society
485 Congress Street
Portland, ME 04111

MARYLAND

Division of Vital Records
State Department of Health
State Office Building
301 West Preston Street
Baltimore, MD 21201

Bureau of Vital Records
City Health Department
Municipal Office Building
Baltimore, MD 21202

Maryland Historical Society
201 West Monument Street
Baltimore, MD 21201

MASSACHUSETTS

Registrar of Vital Statistics
272 State House
Boston, MA 02133

Bay State Historical League
Room 51
The State House
Boston, MA 02133

City Registrar
Registry Division
Health Department
Room 705, City Hall Annex
Boston, MA 02133

Massachusetts Historical Society
1154 Boylston Street
Boston, MA 02115

MICHIGAN

Vital Records Section
Michigan Department of Health
3500 North Logan Street
Lansing, MI 48914

Historical Society of Michigan
2117 Washtenaw Avenue
Ann Arbor, MI 48104

MINNESOTA

Section of Vital Statistics
State Department of Health
350 State Office Building
St. Paul, MN 55101

Minnesota Historical Society and Library
690 Cedar Street
St. Paul, MN 55101

MISSISSIPPI

Division of Public Health Statistics
State Board of Health
P.O. Box 1700
Jackson, MS 39205

Department of Archives and History
Archive and History Bldg.
Capitol Green
Jackson, MS 39205

Vital Records Registration Unit
State Board of Health
P.O. Box 1700
Jackson, MS 39205

MISSOURI

Vital Records
Division of Health
State Department of Public Health and Welfare
Jefferson City, MO 65101

State Historical Society of Missouri
University Library Building
Hitt and Lowry Streets
Columbia, MO 55201

MONTANA

Division of Records and Statistics
State Department of Health
Helena, MT 59601

Montana Historical Society
225 North Roberts Street
Helene, MT 59601

NEBRASKA

Bureau of Vital Statistics
State Department of Health
State Capitol
Lincoln, NE 68509

Nebraska State Historical Society
1500 R Street
Lincoln, NE 68508

NEVADA .

Department of Health, Welfare, and
  Rehabilitation
Division of Health
Section of Vital Statistics
Carson City, NV 89701

Nevada State Historical Society and Library
P.O. Box 1129
Reno, NV 89504

NEW HAMPSHIRE

Department of Health and Welfare
Division of Public Health
Bureau of Vital Statistics
61 South Spring Street
Concord, NH 03301

New Hampshire Historical Society and Library
30 Park Street
Concord, NH 03301

NEW JERSEY

State Department of Health
Bureau of Vital Statistics
P.O. Box 1540
Trenton, NJ 08625

New Jersey Historical Society
240 Broadway
Newark, NJ 07104

New Jersey State Library
Archives and History Bureau
185 W. State St.
Trenton, NJ 06618

NEW MEXICO

Vital Records
New Mexico Health and Social Services
  Department
PERA Building
Room 118
Santa Fe, NM 87501

Museum of New Mexico
P.O. Box 2087
Santa Fe, New Mexico 87501

NEW YORK

Bureau of Vital Records
State Department of Health
Albany, NY 12208

New York Public Library
American History and Genealogy Division
Fifth Avenue and 42nd Street
New York, NY 10018

New York State Historical Association
Lake Road
Cooperstown, NY 13326

NORTH CAROLINA

Public Health Statistics Section
State Board of Health
P.O. Box 2091
Raleight, NC 27602

Division of Archives
Office of Archives and History
State Department of Art, Culture and History
109 E. Jones St.
Raleigh, NC 27611

NORTH DAKOTA

Division of Vital Statistics
State Department of Health
Bismarck, ND 58501

State Historical Society of North Dakota
Liberty Memorial Building
Bismarck, ND 58501

OHIO

Division of Vital Statistics
State Department of Health
G-20 State Department Building
Columbus, OH 43215

Ohio Historical Society
North High Street and 15th Avenue
Columbus, OH 43210

OKLAHOMA

Division of Statistics
State Department of Health
3400 North Eastern
Oklahoma City, OK 73105

Oklahoma Historical Society
Historical Building
Oklahoma City, OK 73105

State D.A.R. Library
Historical Bldg.
Oklahoma City, OK 73105

OREGON

Vital Statistics Section
State Board of Health
P.O. Box 231
Portland, OR 97207

Oregon Historical Society
1230 S.W. Park Avenue
Portland, OR 97205

Oregon State Archives
1005 Broadway, N.E.
Salem, OR 97301

PENNSYLVANIA

Division of Vital Statistics
State Department of Health
Health and Welfare Building
P.O. Box 90
Harrisburg, PA 17120

Pennsylvania Historical and Museum Commission
Div. of Archives
Box 1026
Harrisburg, PA 17108

RHODE ISLAND

Division of Vital Statistics
State Department of Health
State Office Building
Room 351
Providence, RI 02903

Rhode Island Historical Society
52 Powell Street
Providence, RI 02903

Rhode Island State Archives
314 State House
Providence, RI 02900

SOUTH CAROLINA

Bureau of Vital Statistics
State Board of Health
Sims Building
Columbia, SC 29201

South Carolina Department of Archives and
   History
1430 Senate Street
Columbia, SC 29201

SOUTH DAKOTA

Division of Public Health Statistics
State Department of Health
Pierre, SD 57501

South Dakota Historical Society and Library
Memorial Building
Pierre, SD 57501

TENNESSEE

Division of Vital Statistics
State Department of Public Health
Cordell Hull Building
Nashville, TN 37219

Tennessee State Library and Archives
403 7th Ave. N.
Nashville, TN 37219

TEXAS

Bureau of Vital Statistics
State Department of Health
410 East Fifth Street
Austin, TX 78701

Dallas Public Library
Texas History and Genealogy Department
1954 Commerce St.
Dallas, TX 75201

Texas State Historical Association
Box 8059
University Station
Austin, TX 78712

UTAH

Division of Vital Statistics
Utah State Department of Health
44 Medical Drive
Salt Lake City, UT 84113

Genealogical Library
Genealogical Society of the Church of Jesus
  Christ of Latter Day Saints
50 E. North Temple
Salt Lake City, UT 84105

Utah State Historical Society and Library
603 East South Temple
Salt Lake City, UT 84111

VERMONT

Secretary of State
Vital Records Department
State House
Montpellier, VT 05602

Genealogical Library
Bennington Museum
Bennington, VT 05201

Vermont Historical Society and Library
State Administration Building
Montpellier, VT 05602

VIRGINIA

Bureau of Vital Records and Statistics
State Department of Health
James Madison Building
P.O. Box 1000
Richmond, VA 23208

Virginia Historical Society and Library
428 North Blvd.
P.O. Box 7311
Richmond, VA 23221

WASHINGTON

Genealogical Library
1101 2nd S. East
Quincy, WA 98848

Bureau of Vital Statistics
Division of Health
Washington State Department of Social and
  Health Services
Olympia, WA 98501

Washington State Historical Society and Library
315 North Stadium Way
Tacoma, WA 98403

WEST VIRGINIA

Division of Vital Statistics
State Department of Health
State Office Building No. 3
Charleston, WV 25311

Department of Archives and Historical Library
Cultural Center
Capitol Complex
State of West Virginia Library
Charleston, WV 25305

WISCONSIN

Bureau of Health Statistics
Wisconsin Division of Health
P.O. Box 309
Madison, WI 53701

State Historical Society of Wisconsin
816 State Street
Madison, WI 53706

WYOMING

Bureau of Vital Statistics
State Department of Public Health
State Office Building
Cheyenne, WY 82001

Western History and Archives Department
University of Wyoming
Laramie, WY 82070

Wyoming State Historical Society
State Office Building
Cheyenne, WY 82001